W9-DBB-890

See for Yourself

Flowers

See for Yourself

Flowers

Karen Bryant-Mole
Photographs by Barrie Watts

RSVP

RAINTREE
STECK-VAUGHN
PUBLISHERS
The Steck-Vaughn Company

Austin, Texas

Published by Raintree Steck-Vaughn Publishers, an imprint of Steck-Vaughn Company

Editor: Kathy DeVico
Project Manager: Lyda Guz
Electronic Production: Scott Melcer

All photographs by Barrie Watts except: p. 8 John Shaw/NHPA; p. 19 Stephen Dalton/NHPA; p. 23 Martin Wendler/NHPA.

Library of Congress Cataloging-in-Publication Data
Bryant-Mole, Karen.
  Flowers / Karen Bryant-Mole; photographs by Barrie Watts.
     p.   cm. — (See for yourself)
  Includes index.
  ISBN 0-8172-4211-2
    1. Flowers—Juvenile literature.   2. Angiosperms—Juvenile literature.   [1. Flowers.   2. Angiosperms.]   I. Watts, Barrie, ill.
  II. Title.   III. Series.
  QK49.B853   1996
  582.13′04463—dc20   95-31132
                                             CIP
                                             AC

Printed and bound in the United States
1 2 3 4 5 6 7 8 9 0 99 98 97 96 95

Contents

Flowers Everywhere!

Don't these roses look beautiful?
Many plants are grown just for their flowers.
You can see them in gardens or at the florist.

But most plants have some sort of flower.
The plant in the picture below is a tomato plant.
Can you see its small, yellow flowers?
This plant isn't grown for its flowers.
After the flowers die, tomatoes will grow on the plant.

Flowering Trees and Grasses

Trees are the largest of all the flowering plants.
Even though they are the biggest plants,
they often have some of the smallest flowers.
Some trees have flowers that don't really look like flowers.

You can see alder tree flowers in the big picture.
These flowers are called catkins.

Even grasses have flowers.
The grass in lawns and in parks
is usually cut by lawn mowers.
It does not get a chance
to flower. But in meadows,
the grass is left to grow
and to flower.

The meadow grasses
in this picture have
hundreds of tiny flowers
on each stem.

Stems and Leaves

Most flowering plants have a long stalk, called a stem.
Some plants only have one stem.
Other plants, such as the dandelion shown in the big picture, have lots of stems.

Most plants grow roots underground.
Their roots take in water from the soil.

Leaves grow on the stems of plants. Can you see how the leaves of these sunflowers are spread out to catch as much sunlight as possible?

Flowering plants have to make food for themselves. To do this, they use water that is drawn up from the soil by their roots, and air and sunlight that are taken in by their leaves.

Flower Parts

A flower is made up of lots of different parts.

Around the outside of the flower are the petals.

The middle of the flower is where new seeds are made. There are male parts, called stamens. The female parts are called stigmas and ovaries.

Look closely at the middle of this lily. You will see a thick stalk with a red part on the top. This red part is the lily's stigma. The stalk leads down to the ovary. All around the stigma are more stalks. These are the stamens.

Find some flowers, and see if you can name the different parts.

Pollen

Stamens make a special powder, called pollen.
Pollen is usually yellow, orange, or red.
Can you see the pollen on the stamens of this tulip?

Flowering plants need pollen. They use it to make
seeds, from which new plants will grow.

You could collect some pollen from the
stamens of a flower. Use a cotton-tipped swab.
What does the pollen look like?

Before the plant can make new seeds, pollen from the
stamens has to reach the stigma of a plant of the same kind.
This is called pollination.

Try brushing the pollen
you collected over the
stigma of another flower
of the same kind.
You might be helping
to make a new flower.

Helpful Insects

Pollen is spread from flower to flower in different ways.

This bee has landed on a daisy. Pollen is sticking to its legs.
When it flies to another daisy, the pollen may rub off
onto the other daisy's stigmas.

Many plants smell good or are brightly colored in order
to attract insects. Inside the flowers there is sweet-tasting nectar
that the insects like to drink.

Find a small bed of flowers.
Write down the color of
each flower on a chart.
Make a check mark by
the right color each time
an insect visits a flower.

Which colors are the
most popular?

Pollen Spread by the Wind

Most grasses and many trees are pollinated by the wind.
Can you see the pollen being blown off these grass flowers?

Wind-pollinated plants usually make lots of pollen.
With any luck, at least some of this pollen will be blown
onto another plant of the same type.

Wind-pollinated plants often
have small, dull-colored
flowers. They don't need
to attract insect visitors.

Look at the small picture.
See if you can guess
which of these plants are
wind-pollinated, and which
are pollinated by insects.

Where Seeds Grow

After a grain of pollen has landed on a stigma,
the plant may start to grow seeds.
The seeds will grow inside the ovary.

Look at the big picture of a daffodil. It has been cut in half.
Can you see the little seeds inside, waiting to grow?

Some flowers, like the poppy, have lots and lots of tiny seeds.
Others, like the flower of the horse chestnut tree,
have one very large seed.

Ask an adult to cut a flower
in half for you, and see if you
can find some seeds.

Spreading Seeds

When the seeds are ripe, it is time for them to leave the plant.

Many seeds, like these thistle seeds, are spread by the wind. The wind blows them to nearby ground, where one day they may start to grow as new plants.

Animals help to spread seeds, too. Seeds get caught in their coats and drop out later. This squirrel is eating seeds. Often squirrels bury seeds as a food store. Sometimes they forget where they have buried them. So the seeds may start to sprout.

People also help to spread seeds. Can you find out some of the ways that we do this?

Wildflowers

Have you ever been to the countryside and noticed all the wildflowers that grow there?

Many of the plants in our yards have to be looked after. But wildflowers do not need to be cared for at all. Sometimes, hundreds of wildflowers grow in the same place, like the buttercups shown in the big picture.

You can make your own wildflower garden by collecting seeds from wildflowers. Wait until all the petals have dropped off, and the flower head looks old and dry. Shake the flower head into a small bag. If the seeds are ripe, they will drop easily into the bag.

Scatter the seeds on a patch of bare soil, and see what grows there next year.

When Do Flowers Bloom?

Different flowers bloom at different times of the year.
These snowdrops are flowering, even though
it is a cold, wintry day.

What season is it right now?
Make a list of the flowers that are in bloom.
Write down what colors they are, too.
Do you notice anything that is similar about them?

Most spring flowers are yellow.
Summer flowers are often very bright in color.
Many fall flowers are pink or purple.
And the best-known winter flower,
the snowdrop, is white.

Look at the flowers that
the children are holding.
When do you think
these flowers
were in bloom?

More Things to Do

1. Press flowers.
Put your flower between two sheets of waxed paper.
Put a book underneath your flower in its paper. Then
put several books on top. Leave it for a few weeks. You
can use pressed flowers to make birthday cards or gifts.

2. Watch a plant grow toward the sun.
Put a flowering plant on a sunny windowsill. Leaves
need as much sunlight as they can get in order to
make food for the plant. After a few days, you will
notice that the flower and its leaves will be growing
toward the sunlight.

3. Growing flowers
You could use an old bucket to make a tub to grow
flowers in. Ask an adult to cut a small hole in the base.
Put a layer of stones in the bottom, and fill the tub
with soil. Plant flower seeds that are easy to grow,
such as nasturtiums.

4. Flower clocks
Flowers open and close at different times of the day.
Some flowers close up their petals when the air
becomes damp, to protect their pollen from rain
and dew. Look at some flowers in your school
playground or in a yard. When do they open
and close?

Index

This index will help you find some
of the important words in this book.

Notes for Parents and Teachers

These notes will give you some additional information about flowering plants and suggest more activities you could try with children.

Pages 6–7

Plants can be divided into two groups: flowering plants and nonflowering plants. Flowering plants are plants that produce covered seeds. The flowering plant group is by far the larger. Nonflowering plants include lichens, algae, and ferns. Most nonflowering plants reproduce by producing spores.

Pages 8–9

The grass family includes cereals, like wheat, barley, and oats. All grasses have some features in common. They have hollow stems with nodes, or joints. The leaves grow alternately on the stem. The leaves are generally long and narrow. Grass flowers are usually green.

Pages 10–11

Plants draw water up from the soil through their roots. The water is then taken up to the leaves through narrow tubes in the stem, called xylem. Children can see this for themselves by placing a stalk of celery in some water colored with ink, and leaving the stalk in the colored water for a day. When they break open the stalk of celery, they will see that the tubes in the stem have been colored by the ink as it traveled upward. Leaves contain a special substance, called chlorophyll. This captures the energy in sunlight. Plants use this energy to turn carbon dioxide from the air and water from the soil into carbohydrates and oxygen. This process is called photosynthesis.

Pages 12–13

The male flower parts, called stamens, are made up of stalks, called filaments, and anthers, which are the pollen sacs. Female flower parts also have individual and group names. The stigma and ovary are generally joined by a style. The stigma, style, and ovary are known as the carpel. A group of carpels that are fused together are called a pistil. Some plants have several separate carpels. Each one of these can be called a pistil. Although most flowers have both male and female parts, some flowering plants, like the alder tree, have separate female flowers and male flowers. A few flowering plants, like the willow, grow their male flowers and female flowers on completely separate plants.

Pages 14–17

Some flowers can reproduce by using their own pollen. This is called self-pollination. Others need to receive pollen from another flower of the same kind—cross-pollination. One of the main functions of a flower's petals is to guide visiting pollinators to the center of the flower head. Many insects are pollinators. Children could watch a bed of flowers and see how many different insects visit it.

Pages 24–25

Wildflowers grow easily because they are growing in conditions that are ideal for that variety of plant. If seeds are collected in one area and planted in another, some varieties may grow more successfully than others. However, if children collect a range of seeds, some should grow well.